Hail Mary: woman, wife, Mother of God

James Breig

Illustrated by Pat Doyle

Credits: Design, Glenn Heinlein; Illustrations, Pat Doyle.

ISBN: 0-89570-197-9

First printing, August 1980

Claretian Publications

Hail Mary: woman, wife, Mother of God

James Breig

Hail, Mary

Along the edge of her hand ran a callus, a bumpy ridge of hard flesh, raised by countless hours of pounding her palm against the resilient dough which lay on the hardwood table her husband had fashioned. She was small, barely rising to her husband's shoulder, and her son was nearing a promised goal of his childhood: topping his mother's height when they stood back-to-back. Her hands were small, too, with thin fingers that ached from kneading the flour into loaves to feed her family.

She wondered about the callus and how it felt to her husband when she took his large, rough hand in hers at the end of the day. She wondered how many times her son had—undetected, he thought—let his fingers wander to that spot to feel the cracks and hardness. His own soft palm was being blistered more and more lately as he learned the intricacies of the plane. He and his father would come home every evening, their hair matted with sweat from the day's heat, their clothes covered with shavings and sawdust, laughing over something and eager to tell her.

Her own day was filled with other chores—the three goats in the pen had to be tended to, water had to be brought up the hill three times a day, cloaks had to be washed and washed again against the rocks in the stream, dinner had to be prepared. . .

Along the nail of her thumb ran a crack, dividing the nail into two parts, one side thick and horny, the other side smooth. She had split it one day holding down the goat when it had taken a fever and begun thrashing about in the pen, its horns threatening the other two, which bleated their fear, blood already flecking the side of one. Her husband and son were gone, eyeing a tree, seeing in its trunk the lines of a

5

wagon tongue. They had returned to find her exhausted and drained, her shoulders throbbing from the battle. That night, they had pounded the dough against the table's planking and whispered their admiration while she slept.

Her husband, between chews of their unsuccessful bread and herbs, widened the eyes of their son with other stories about her. How such perseverance and strength welled from so small a person puzzled them both.

Her son, his plate of food untouched before him, was captivated with the stories about the donkey-borne woman who half walked, half rode over the mountains while he rested inside her, about the woman who had seen so much and feared so little.

Along the weathered skin of her arm ran a two-inch scar, a slight ripple in her forearm, left by a briar's needle. It had punctured her and she had pulled back without thinking, ripping open the flesh. Her son's face had gone white when he saw the injury, and he stumbled in his hurry to get help, sprawling face-first into a mud puddle. The sight of him brought a smile to her lips which she tried to hide so his pride wouldn't be hurt. Forgetting her arm, she helped him to his feet and wiped his face and hands with her sleeve. His eyes stayed glued to her arm where the blood was drying quickly. She had forgotten the throbbing long before they got home, where he so carefully (and so ineptly) cleaned her wound and bandaged it.

Daily he would check his handiwork, lifting the cloth to peek under. Finally he pronounced her healthy and removed the bandage, revealing the pink line of the scar. Everytime she washed, her fingers paused a moment at the little line that the briar had made, and she smiled secretly at the memory of the mud-boy.

The smile played on her thin lips, which were like her father's, and crinkled her long nose, which was a copy of her mother's. Her long, dark hair, she told herself again and again, came from both her parents. It was a tangle of brown and black strands, some curly, some stringy. As a result, it was impossible to tame. She had long since given up trying

6

and counted as a plus the extra minutes a day she saved by not having to comb and primp it. A few quick strokes with her fingers and it was in place.

Her name was Mary—closer to the original—perhaps we had better say, Miriam. She was a woman, a real person, a human being like us. She did not wear blue or carry a rosary. She did not stand on globes and crush serpents with her heel. She was not a movie star in looks or attitude. She was something less than her worshippers would believe and something more than her detractors would wish.

If she did not have a callus on her hand, a split nail, or a scar on her arm, it is likely her body reflected in some way the hard life she lived, the life of any woman of her time. She was not a fairy princess, protected from the harshness of the weather and the demands of daily chores. Perhaps her arms were muscled from lifting water jugs; perhaps her face was cracked and dry from the Middle East sun.

Whatever the facts of her personal appearance, one thing is certain: She was the mother of Jesus Christ. For that, she has been remembered for 2000 years. The memory has been at times heretical (there were some who worshipped her as a god), at times romanticized (the chivalric code was dedicated to her), at times dim (after the Second Vatican Council, said Father Patrick Peyton, the rosary priest, Mary went into "an eclipse"). But the memory has stayed, no matter how it has been twisted or fogged.

Who was Mary? What is her role in Christ's life? In the life of the church? In our lives today? Is she still relevant? These are some of the questions we will be examining in coming chapters as we get to know this woman better and better.

Full of grace

There is no one key to understanding Mary. The complexity of a human being can never be reduced to one simple formula. Hamlet was more than an indecisive man; Ahab's psyche encased more than monomania; there was more to Joan of Arc than voices. The wonder, mystery, and beauty of any person is his or her complexity. Diamonds are prized for their facets, each one a different angle, each one a new reflection. So it is with people. So it is with Mary.

One facet is her freedom. The phrase *full of grace* testifies to her freedom, for we are grace-filled (that is, close to God) only to the degree that we are free. When we chain ourselves to things, when we limit our freedom, when we tie ourselves down, we inhibit our closeness to the Creator.

Mary knew no chains. She lived as God intends us all to live—perfectly free. In creating us, God refused to bind us to his will; we are not made as puppets to jump to his string-pulling. He made us capable of choices, even the choice of rejecting him. No puppet ever turned against its maker; such a rebellion is ridiculous even to imagine, so in control is the puppeteer. Not so with God, who made us free. Our choice can lead us astray or take us back to him, back to grace.

Mary's choice was God. It was a choice she made freely, even blindly. When God called on her, she did not understand what he wanted her to do, but she acquiesced. She selected her answer, not because she was forced to, but because she wanted to.

I have often wondered if others were offered the same choice. Had an angel of the Lord gone to other women throughout history asking them to bear God's son? Had others heard the request and turned it down? Had others been called, only to answer no? Had the angel come to us, what would our answer have been? More realistically, when God comes to us now, what is our answer?

In her response to God, Mary is a model for us. She trusted God, she placed her faith in him blindly, she assented to him with the hope that he would not fail her. Ahead of her lay difficulties, but she was willing to face them as long as God stood with her.

Willing. It is a central word in the life of Mary. To be willing is to be free. When you say, "I am willing to do that," you are not saying, "I am forced to do that," or "I am required to do that." You are making a free decision.

To say that Mary was full of grace is not to state that something was poured into her, but to attest to something she was. She was grace-filled as a result of her choices. In turn, her choices could be made more freely as she became more and more grace-filled (closer and closer to God).

At the Annunciation Mary chose God freely and with trust in his faithfulness to her. That choice was renewed throughout her life: at the Visitation, at Christ's birth, at the Presentation, when her son was lost in the Temple, during the hidden years, at the wedding feast at Cana, during Jesus' ministry, in the dark days of his death, in the triumph of his Resurrection, during the final years of her life.

Again and again, faced with a choice, she freely turned to God. She could have said no to the angel, she could have railed against God when her son suffered, she could have despaired in the upper room after his death. Instead she willed to follow God's wisdom and promise in everything she did. In her room with the angel, in the cold stable of Bethlehem, along the road to Egypt, on the streets of Jerusalem, atop the hill of Calvary, within the tomb of Jesus, inside the room of fear before the Resurrection—in all these places, she had choices; in all these places, she could have said, "Not this time"; in all these places, she could have opted for terror, doubt, hopelessness, or despair. But she did not. At each point, she freely chose God's way.

Some people would say that God's way is not the way of freedom or that it is easy to follow his wishes or that he forces the choice. Such people have not considered the lives of others in the Old and New Testament (not to mention the 20 centuries since then) who, faced with a road that diverged God's way and another way, walked the latter path.

Mary always turned God's way, which is not always the easy way, as her suffering proved. She knew cold and hunger, puzzlement and loss, poverty and bereavement, pain and death. None of that deterred her, however, from freely following God the next time a choice was offered.

The next time. The next time we choose for or against God is every day. In each act we perform, we are declaring ourselves—with our free will—for or against God. A decision against God may lead us to riches, fame, and domination over others, while a decision for him may take us to deprivation, abandonment, and loneliness. Mary's life tells us that we should not base our decision on such temporal grounds. Her free choices brought her pain in her son's torture and death, but, knowing her ultimate reward, who would not choose the same?

Or would we, more realistically, make our choices based on immediate rewards? Like Peter, who chose safety and denied Christ? Like Judas, who chose money and sold Christ? Like us, who choose immediate comforts (wealth, security, friendships, promotions) and reject God's way?

Mary's life can show us another way, a way more difficult at first but more fulfilling in the end. A way, incidentally, which brought her more freedom by opening her up to God and releasing her from the chains and ropes which so often bind us.

She chose obscurity to fame and shed the shackle of celebrity; she chose poverty to wealth and removed the weight of greed; she chose God over all else and threw off the handcuffs of this world: temptation, sin, vice, corruption.

This woman—perhaps with calloused hands, broken nails, and scarred arms—this woman, as human as each of us, did what all of us are invited to do: freely choose God. That she could do it, faced with all the troubles of her life, proves that we can too.

The Lord is with thee

All that we know about Mary, our model, is contained in a few passages in the New Testament. While some Old Testament references can be applied to her role as Jesus' mother, they do not tell us anything about her personally. In addition, traditions have grown up about her in the 20 centuries since her death. But they are either pious fictions meant for inspiration or deliberate lies intended to downgrade her.

For the truth of her, we can turn only to the Gospels and one reference in the Acts of the Apostles. What is interesting to discover is that, while references to her are few, they are revelatory of a multifaceted personality.

• At the Annunciation, she is the obedient child of God, filled with awe and wonder at the angel's words, ready to do the Lord's will but not so docile that she does not ask, "How can this be?"
• With Joseph, she is loving and understanding, patient with his bewilderment, trusting that he will trust her.
• In going to Elizabeth, she displays a concern for others that ignores her own pregnancy. She sacrifices her comfort to be at the side of her cousin. This same selfless disregard for her own ease is displayed again in her journey to Bethlehem and again when she flees to Egypt.
• The words of Simeon must have terrified her, and her son's declaration that he had to be about his father's work must have confounded her. During the hidden years of Jesus' adolescence, amid the normal joys and pains of raising a child, Mary must have experienced special pangs as the realization of her son's future dawned upon her. Perhaps she grew possessive of him, wanting to stay with him as long as possible. Perhaps that is why, at Cana, Jesus is surprised

13

when Mary tells him to, in effect, begin his public life. She is letting him go into the world.

• It was a letting go that would seemingly end on Calvary where she proved herself to be stronger than all but one of the Apostles. Her faith in the Lord's promise at the Annunciation did not break when she saw her son die; it did not shatter in the upper room; it did not collapse when the tomb was found empty.

In these passages from the Gospels, she goes from being a puzzled young girl asked to carry out the work of God to a strong-willed woman who sees that work fulfilled. She displays humility in the face of her role; she is at times worried (over her lost child) and at times no doubt hurt (by her son's question, "Who is my mother?"), but she is never defeated.

Throughout her life, she relied on the Lord. He remained with her all her days:

in Nazareth the day the angel came (Luke 1:26);
in the hill country when she visited Elizabeth (Luke 1:39);
in Bethlehem's stable for the birth of her child (Luke 2:4,7; Matt. 2:1);
in Jerusalem for her purification and the child's offering to Yahweh (Luke 2:22);
in Nazareth later for the child's early days (Luke 2:51; Matt. 2:23);
in Jerusalem in the Temple when Jesus was lost (Luke 2:42, 46);
in Cana for the wedding feast (John 2:1);
on Calvary (John 19:25).

At each phase of her life, the Lord was with Mary, not as a glued-on extra but as an invited guest. God did not impose himself on her, but asked if he could enter her life. To which she responded with a yes that has changed the history of the world.

Mary predicted 2000 years ago that "henceforth, all nations shall call me blessed." Indeed throughout history and across the globe, she has been known as the Blessed Virgin and Blessed Mother, literal examples of how accurate her assessment was.

She was blessed because God came into her life. She was blessed because she opened herself to him. Again, she stands as a model for us of how we can respond to the call from God. He speaks, we listen; he knocks, we open; he reaches out, we take him in. Most intimately, in the act of conceiving the Messiah, Mary did these things. It was a union we are all invited to join.

Blessed art thou
among women

That Mary was a woman has proved to be both an asset and a liability.

For centuries, those people who wished to relegate women to a background role, whether in the church or in society at large, appealed to their image of Mary. They pointed to the humble and obedient Mary, the homemaker Mary, the wife and mother Mary, the Mary who stayed in the shadows of her son.

Lately, on the other hand, those people who wish to claim for women an equal place in the church and society have trotted out another image. They call on the Mary who freely chose her role in salvation history, Mary the bold at Cana, Mary the strong on Calvary.

As we pointed out, Mary's appealing complexity has allowed for a multitude of interpretations of her as a symbol. Author Mary Carson has mixed feelings about Mary as the model for contemporary feminists but recognizes that she radiates "an image for each individual according to what they need her to be. She had a diverse personality. She was a mother, the woman who started Christ's ministry, and so on. You can find a model for almost anything you need."

What would Mary—the Mary of the calloused hands, the real Mary—have thought about this tug-of-war over her image? Since these varied aspects existed in her single personality, we might guess she would be astonished at the debate. After all, these aspects are not contradictions. Housewifery is not the antithesis of leadership, despite the battle lines drawn by many current ideologues. Humility need not be interpreted as submission nor motherhood as submersion.

The beauty of Mary—the beauty of any woman—is that she is an individual, a unique creation encapsuling many different facets, some of which may, if seen narrowly, seem paradoxical. (Surprise: This is also the beauty of any man.) In her life, Mary acted many roles. The retiring mother of Nazareth could become the leader in the upper room; the gentle girl in Bethlehem could become the decisive friend determined to visit Elizabeth despite all obstacles; the obedient wife of Joseph could become his guide to understanding the will of God.

To select just one side of this list and proclaim that it captures the essence of Mary is to be blind to the complete woman she is. To hold her up as a symbol of this or that movement (and, in the process, ignore her many facets) is to cheapen her as a person. To reduce this complex person to the level of a cliche is to exploit her.

Mary is not a trademark to be used as a shorthand way of gaining sympathy. To use her thus reduces her to the level of the cartoon characters who sell hamburgers and soup. Looking at her, we should see not a logo for some movement but a singular human being. (How much, by way of comparison, has Abraham Lincoln suffered by the use of his face to sell insurance? How much of his complexity is trampled when he becomes a password for an automobile?)

Unless we approach Mary as a real person (she of the scarred arm), we will miss all that she has to offer us in example, guidance, and solace. Symbols do not understand our feelings; logos do not respond to our entreaties; catchphrases do not comfort us. Mary is not a cliche any more than each of us is. To treat her as one crushes her individuality and ruins any chance of establishing with her a relationship of trust and confidence.

Mary was a woman. That is neither a brand of shame nor a badge of honor. More important, Mary was Mary. Her womanhood, along with her place of birth, her parents, her intelligence, capacity, and dozens of other factors contributed to her being Mary. Mary's womanhood was part of her life, not its sum total. Those who treat her as only a woman—either a quietly submissive one or a boldly pioneering one—are cheating themselves of her completeness, her mary-ness.

She was not an insipid wife nor a militant feminist. She was Mary, and that is much more than anyone else can ever comprehend.

And blessed is the fruit of thy womb, Jesus

For a person who lived within a few square miles of one point most of her life, for a person whose influence during her life reached only a handful, for a person concerned with the simplest of life's problems and its most basic trials, Mary has had an enormous, worldwide impact and has been the subject of some very difficult theological questions. In the process she has often been lost. In the swirl of debate over such matters as the Immaculate Conception, the virgin birth, and her role in redemption, Mary is sometimes forgotten.

All this results, of course, from the fact that she was the mother of Jesus Christ. That God chose the Incarnation (the emptying of his divinity to become human) as the means of our salvation required the cooperation of Mary. This nexus of the human and the divine has proved to be a fusion from which has exploded some of the most intense theological ponderings.

For example, if God was to be born of a woman, what sort of woman would his mother be? Could his mother be a sinner? Could she be capable of sinning? If not, could she be truly human or would she be some sort of ethereal creature, out of touch with our condition? The church's answer is the Immaculate Conception, the dogma that teaches that Mary was conceived herself without original sin and, therefore, without the leaning toward sin which plagues the remainder of humanity.

But the puzzle remains: Did this make her more free to answer God's call or did it make her his puppet, automatically disposed to accept her role?

Another question: Would the son of God be born as a

result of the normal union of man and woman or would he be conceived from the union of God and woman? The doctrine of the virgin birth (and Mary's perpetual virginity) holds that Christ was conceived from the mystical union of the Spirit and Mary and that she never engaged in sexual intercourse.

But others see a different solution. They find this answer a problem because it implies that Jesus was not fully human. As one Protestant thinker put it: "The greatest problem of the virgin birth is that it threatens the real humanity of Jesus. Can he be like his brethren in every respect if he came into the world in a very abnormal way?"

Then there is the question of Mary's role in redemption. As Christ's mother, she brought the Savior into the world. That is obvious. But was her role more extensive than that? Mary Carson describes her as "the first priest because she took matter and changed it into the Body and Blood of Christ." Did that act win for her a special place in the work of salvation beyond Jesus' nativity?

Certainly she was more than a physical conduit for Christ's entrance into creation. To reduce her to that would be to place her on the level of the unconscious. But if her role is larger, how large is it? Early heretics were condemned by the church for claiming divinity for Mary herself, for turning her into a fourth person of God. Others have been censured for ignoring her completely.

The answer is provided in obscure terms like *coredemptrix* and *mediatrix,* which translate to this: Mary is a bridge between us and God, not only in that she brought his son into the world but also in that we can approach God through her. Which raises another problem: Can Mary get in the way of Jesus? Can devotion to her be so strong that he is neglected?

The answer is yes. Many people have fallen into the trap of praying exclusively to Mary without regard for her son, basing their spiritual lives on a relationship with her while never advancing beyond that to Jesus. The correct way is to use her as a bridge. She invites us to learn about her son through her, but she constantly points to him.

22

With any celebrity (picture a new president), we can learn about him or her through relatives. They are interviewed again and again about the famous person's past, personality, and beliefs. In the end, however, the interviewers must go to the person to get the real story. So it is with Mary. She can guide us, she can lead us, she can take us on our first steps. In the end, though, we must go past her to Jesus.

"My soul," she affirmed, "magnifies the Lord." In other words, she exists to display him, she exists to spread his message, she exists to show how much a relationship with him will do for a person.

All this debate and theologizing is important. It can help us understand Mary. Unfortunately it can also achieve the opposite. The verbiage can cloud her from us. Tangled in the syntax and subtleties, we can forget the reality of Mary, the Mary of the broken nail.

"I feel this way about dogmas about Mary," said Mary Carson. "They are fine if it's important for a person to believe them. But for me they make no difference. I'm not dependent on dogmas to believe in Mary as a friend. That's my relationship with her. She is not a superhero to me. If a saint is above normal, beyond my strengths and weaknesses, I can't identify with her."

And Mary is not a superhero. Cut away all the complex jargon (Immaculate Conception, virgin birth, mediatrix) and we find the same woman we have been talking about all along. She is Mary.

This is not to deny the importance of theological research and study. It is only to place it in its proper perspective. When it obscures our understanding of Mary, it should be set aside. But when it enhances our understanding of her, it should be embraced.

Holy Mary, Mother of God

When you start listing all the titles Mary is known by (burdened by?), it is a wonder the real person comes through. She trails aliases like a much-honored duke who is known as prince of this and protector of that.

First, there are the "Our Lady of" titles. Mary is Our Lady of Fatima, of Lourdes, of Czestochowa, of Guadalupe. Then she is the Mother of God, Mother of the Church, Mother Most Pure. She's the Lovely Lady Dressed in Blue and Queen of the Angels.

Unravel her litany and there is more: Virgin Most Pure, Spouse of the Holy Spirit, Tower of Ivory, Mystical Rose, Arc of the Covenant.

If there are not enough traditional titles, Bishop Charles Greco, supreme chaplain of the Knights of Columbus, suggests some new ones: "Mary certainly can be called Our Lady of the Dishpan Hands, who constantly cleaned and scoured the little house in Nazareth. She was Our Lady of the Dusty Feet, who several times a day in sandaled feet made the trip to the town well. She was Our Lady of the Aching Shoulders, Our Lady of the Heavy Heart, Our Lady of the Helping Hand, Our Lady in the Background."

There are some who hold that this multiplicity of titles is part of Mary's attractiveness, that they allow each person to see in her something specifically for him or her.

But the opposite might be true as well. Such a variety might turn Mary into a nobody. By being so many different people, she is, in the final analysis, none of them. Being everything to everyone, there is no real Mary underneath. So many split personalities could be the sign of no whole personality at the bottom.

Throughout these pages, the only title used has been her

name, Mary. This is purposeful; it is a means of getting at the real person behind the myths and symbols, at the calloused hands beneath the gorgeous robes, at the broken thumb-nail on the rosary bead.

To an extent, Mary has been drowned in her titles, veiled behind a plethora of pseudonyms which transform her into a regal ruler or a distant object. Similarly her many painted images have hidden her from us. Some would contend that Our Lady of Guadalupe's face appeals to the Hispanics while the serene face of the Lourdes virgin attracts white Americans.

There are hundreds of images of Mary. She is always beautiful, a symbolic representation of her purity. Surrounded by angels, robed in blue, standing on an orb, rosary-draped, she has many faces, each designed for a specific audience, a particular time, a special place.

But they are all misleading. She looked like none of them. They are too easy; they allow us to select an attractive version which pleases us; they do not challenge us.

What if Mary had bad skin? A broken nose? Crooked teeth? Would she be less as a result? If we had a photograph of her, would she appeal to only a small percentage of believers while others, esthetically disappointed, would drift away from her?

Coming to know Mary should not be so easy, so facile, so comfortable. It should require effort and, once achieved, it should be the real Mary we know, not some title or painting. Perhaps the original iconoclasts (image-breakers) had the right idea; perhaps the ancient Jewish proscription against drawing an image of God is best; perhaps there should be no representation of Mary.

Or better yet, perhaps there should be only one. Erase all the others and settle on one. We don't know what she looked like, but let's agree on certain physical characteristics which were likely in her time and place. Then paint one image of her. She will be more real as a result.

There is something about seeing the person that makes him or her more real, more present, more approachable. And eliminate all the extraneous titles. Let her be, simply, Mary.

The titles and images are meant to do her honor, but they may accomplish the opposite. Rather than help us to know her, they divide us from her, placing her at a distance.

Imagine a pen pal. You exchange photos and letters, getting to know her. You establish a relationship.

Imagine another pen pal. With the first letter, he sends you ten photos and says one could be of him. Then he tells you to refer to him in each letter by a different name, one week John, the next Dave, the next Bob.

Which pen pal is closer to you? Which do you know better?

Pinch your cheek, rumple your hair, stamp your foot. Mary is as real as that. She is not an ethereal goddess or a human chameleon. Her name stayed the same for her life and her face did nothing but age. Like you, she was a person, calloused and scarred, a person capable of great things.

Pray for us sinners

Devotion to Mary, ancient records of the church document, began as early as other devotions among Christians. As far back as we can trace, the faithful have turned to her for advice, solace, and protection (in a second century parchment fragment, there appears an early, crude form of what would be more elegantly expressed in the Memorare). Through the centuries, again and again, the church, through its official papal pronouncements and through the action of the faithful, has underlined its belief that devotion to Mary is essential.

Throughout this time, special prayers, such as the Memorare and the Rosary, have been composed especially for her. Days (Saturday), Months (May, October), and even years (the Marian Year of 1954) have been dedicated to her. Different cultures have devised their own unique services to her, such as the Italian celebration of the feast of the Assumption or the Hispanic festival honoring Our Lady of Guadalupe.

Recently the charismatic and the ecumenical movements have been looking into how Mary can be a part of their groups. Carmelite Father Louis Rogge, a theologian at Loyola University in Chicago, has noted that there is "a quickening of interest in Mary" among non-Roman Catholics along with a realization that her role is essential in the divine plan and that the "proclamation of the Good News without her is no longer the full Gospel of Jesus Christ."

Focusing on Mary's relationship to the charismatic movement, Father Rene Laurentin, a noted Marian scholar, feels that she is "a model in her relationship to the Holy Spirit and in her charisms." He sees her as a prototype of the church, "Spirit-led, God-centered, and charismatic."

Whether prayer is addressed to Mary by thousands at shrines to her the world over or by one person, it is a testimony to her place in the church's prayer life.

But why do people pray to her? What do they hope she will do for them? At a time when many traditional devotions have fallen off, why is prayer to Mary still popular; why is it, in fact, increasing in the new movements in the church?

One reason is that the church has clarified its understanding of Mary and placed her more precisely within its understanding of the flow of salvation history. In doing this redefining, the church accomplished two significant and almost antithetical things. It attracted new people to Marian devotion while not losing those who had been there all along. By placing Mary in her proper place and relationship to the Trinity, by deciding when prayer to her was appropriate and when not (no rosaries at Mass, for example), the church attracted non-Roman Catholics (heretofore distrustful of the exalted, near-divine place given to Mary) and the post-Vatican II Catholics while not offending her traditional devotees.

Those who charged that she had been downgraded by the Second Vatican Council soon came to realize that the Council's definitions clarified rather than demeaned Mary's role. (It was, after all, the Council Fathers who urged "all children of the church" to "generously foster" devotion to Mary. The Council clearly stated its aim of keeping the traditional while attracting the avante-garde when it stressed that care be taken to avoid "the falsity of exaggeration on the one hand and the excess of narrowmindedness on the other" when it came to examining the dignity of Mary.)

Prayer to Mary is an ancient and modern thing. It is practiced by traditional means (the Rosary is still broadcast weekly on dozens of radio stations across the nation) and by more contemporary ones. ("All I do," revealed a woman, "is talk to her about my problems. There is nothing formal about it.") In little Italies, fireworks bang on the Assumption; in barrios, mariachis trumpet Guadalupe while, in charismatic prayer groups, upraised arms praise her.

The style of prayer is always an individual matter. People select their prayer modes (and one is never sufficient; a variety is needed) to suit their needs at different times. Alone, they choose private prayers; in the home, a group devotion, but one that is still intimate, is preferred; in a church or other setting, still another style is required.

What is essential is that a relationship to Mary be established through the intimate conversation of prayer. Her life and personality prove that she has much to offer us in terms of comfort, aid, counsel, and encouragement. There is nothing we can undergo, no pain we can experience, no loss we can know that she will not sympathize with.

As Jesuit Father Charles Gallagher put it, "We really need to be close to Mary, not just to discover her goodness but to discover our own. . . . She treats us exactly the way she treated Jesus back in Nazareth, with the same love, enthusiasm, joy, and tenderness."

Mary is our mother, embodying all the positive qualities of parenting. She is concerned about us, as she was about the lost boy in the Temple; she is thinking about us always, as she pondered all things in her heart; she is confident in our ability, as she was about Jesus at Cana; she is a strong woman, as Calvary proved, ready to withstand the worst in order to reach the salvation ahead.

Often portrayed as sticky-sweet, she no doubt possessed much more complex emotions. Like all parents, she could mix sternness with her love, disappointment with her encouragement, anger with her pride. She has at her command all the tools to raise us into adult Christians, to lead us from our infant faith through a period of adolescent growth to our goal of a complete and mature faith.

Whatever it takes, she will do—if we ask her. She does not impose herself on us any more than God imposed himself on her. Rather, like him, she invites us to utilize her strengths, to find in her a guide to spiritual fulfillment.

We answer that invitation in prayer, in our simple dialog with her, in an exchange that involves listening as well as speaking.

Now and at the hour
of our death

The Rosary remains the most famous of all prayers to Mary.
The repetition of the Hail Mary, whether Catholics knew it
or not, reflected a Zen style of meditation. Through the
familiarity that comes with repetition, the person praying
has more freedom to reflect on the words and to delve fur-
ther into his or her relationship with God.

The beads lost some of their value in the wake of the Second Vatican Council when some people found them to be
relics of the past, more symbolic of the immigrant church in
America than a valid means of prayer. But like so many
things neglected in those tumultuous, post-Council years, the
Rosary is returning to favor as more and more people find it
to be a simple, meditative prayer style which has the added
advantage of being convenient (it's portable, after all).

And one young Catholic, a recent college graduate, dis-
covered that the Rosary can also be flexible. "I grew up saying the Rosary with my family every night," he said, "and it
became very boring. The same prayers every night. But last
year I tried something new. I used the rosary for other
prayers. Sometimes I would recite familiar prayers using the
beads to count them; other times I would write my own
prayer and recite it. The beads, when you think about them,
are like computers. They help you keep track and they
discipline you to stick to your prayers. You can't skimp and
say to yourself that you're going to skip prayers today.
You've got to follow the rosary from beginning to end.
That's why I have returned to it. It's a way of keeping myself
on track with my prayer life."

The rosary is a visible sign of devotion to Mary. There are others. The miraculous medal, for example, is worn by millions of people around the world while still more wear scapulars. These, too, faded from favor after the Council. But recent reports declare they are returning as more and more people discover they need something material to remind them of their faith.

"Medals and scapulars declined," explained a priest, "because some came to treat them as magic amulets. Wear them and your troubles were gone. That notion offended people. Now we are rediscovering their worth, not as lucky charms but as reminders to pray and signs of our devotion. We are spiritual and physical beings. We need physical things—medals, bread and wine, candles—to help us grow spiritually."

Whatever appeals to you—the rosary, medals and scapulars, ethnic celebrations such as Our Lady of Charity of Cobre (for Cuban-Americans) and Our Lady of San Juan del Valle (for Puerto Ricans)—the simplest and most often spoken prayer remains the Hail Mary. With its first half drawn from Scripture and its second half a petition, the Hail Mary concludes with a prayer for help at the "hour of our death." No doubt most people recite the Hail Mary with the emphasis on help now, preferring not to think about later. But recent years have brought a new emphasis to the dying process; the veils have been drawn aside, and we have been asked to look at the end of life not as something horrible but as the natural conclusion to earthly existence.

It is perfectly appropriate that Mary should be called on to be with us when we die or when we face the deaths of others. Her life was filled with moments of such crisis. From the slaughter of the innocents to the hill of the Crucifixion, from Simeon's prophecy that a sword would pierce her heart to the burden of her son in her arms on Calvary, Mary faced death with the strength of a woman firm in her faith. She mourned, but she did not cry out against God; she suffered, but she did not collapse into inactivity; she wept, but she did not close her eyes to reality. We can never know how much she understood about death. This woman of the pieta—did she know her son would rise? Did she know that life was everlasting? Did she know that dying was only a passage to a new life? Or did she hold to the Jewish belief in Sheol, an afterlife of shadows? Or was she confused by her son's preaching on the topic?

Perhaps she was an amalgam of all this and more. Whatever her level of understanding, she accepted this from God as she had accepted so much else. She trusted in him.

At moments in our lives when death touches us, we should trust too.

Amen

She wanted to laugh but could not. Not as long as her son
was spinning his story of what had happened that morning in
the shop. But he got such a serious look on his face when
reporting that it made her want to smile in return. She had
that to struggle against as well as the content of the story—
her husband catching his robe in the plane and tearing a hole
in it, then trying to sew it up with a wooden needle their son
had fashioned from scraps. Her son told it with embellish-
ments and hand waves, walking back and forth to indicate
where he and his father stood. It was as though he were con-
veying the greatest news in the world.

She wanted to smile but held it in, knowing she could let it
out later when he had gone to bed and the two of them sat up
to talk about him. The last time the plane had snagged
something, it had been her son's forearm, and he came home
bawling. She lectured him on how 3-year-olds were not to
play with their fathers' tools. Then she kissed the scrape and
his eyes dried up.

She wanted to smile at the memory of those years, but the
teller of tales would think she was laughing at him.

And she would never hurt him.

Her husband came in carrying his arm against his robe in a
funny way, trying to conceal the hole, unaware that the event
was, at that moment, being re-enacted for the person who
would have to make the repairs less clumsily. He nodded to
her and then heard his son's words. With a shrug of chagrin,
he pulled aside his arm and showed the rent, stitched with the
thick string he used to tie wood together.

She wanted to laugh again but instead put her hand near
her mouth and slid a finger across her lips. If she bit it, she
would stifle the urge. Her husband caught the movement and

gave her a look of support. Their son would soon conclude and have to go to the well. They could laugh together then.

He finished with a flourish and took his mother's hand, his fingers, like always, secretly feeling the calloused edge. His face remained serious, awaiting her comment, which she gave with an embrace, pulling him closer so she could smile over his shoulder at her husband who stuck his fingers through the garment's hole and waggled a hello to her.

She was Miriam to them. She is Mary to us. As real as a broken fingernail. As human as a scar on an arm. Proof through the centuries that real people can attain spiritual fulfillment, contentment, and equanimity; evidence that one may be human and still be like God.